Date: 12/14/15

J BIO DAVIS
Fishman, Jon M.,
Anthony Davis /

Anthony Davis

By Jon M. Fishman

AMAZING ATHLETES

Lerner Publications ◆ Minneapolis

Lerner Publications Company
A division of Lerner Publishing Group, Inc.
241 First Avenue North
Minneapolis, MN 55401 USA

For reading levels and more information, look up this title at www.lernerbooks.com.

Library of Congress Cataloging-in-Publication Data

Fishman, Jon M.
  Anthony Davis / by Jon M. Fishman.
    pages cm. — (Amazing Athletes)
  Includes index.
  Includes webography.
  Audience: Age: 7–11.
  Audience: Grade K to Grade 3.
    ISBN 978-1-4677-9367-4 (lb : alk. paper) — ISBN 978-1-4677-9369-8 (pb : alk. paper) —
ISBN 978-1-4677-9370-4 (eb pdf)
    1. Davis, Anthony Marshon, 1993– —Juvenile literature. 2. Basketball players—Illinois—
Chicago—Biography—Juvenile literature 3. New Orleans Hornets (Basketball team)—History—
Juvenile literature. 4. New Orleans Pelicans (Basketball team)—Juvenile literature. I. Title.
  GV884.D37F57 2016
  796.323092—dc23 [B]   2015013878

Manufactured in the United States of America
1 – BP – 7/15/15

TABLE OF CONTENTS

Anthony Davis dunks against the Sacramento Kings early in the 2014–2015 season.

THE PELICAN KING

New Orleans Pelicans **forward** Anthony Davis caught the basketball in both hands. He leaped into the air. Then he raised the ball above the **rim** with his right hand. *Slam!* Anthony stuffed the ball through the hoop for two points.

The Pelicans were playing against the Sacramento Kings on November 18, 2014. The game was in Sacramento, California. The 2014–2015 NBA season had just started a few weeks earlier.

Anthony *(left)* looks for a shot around Jason Thompson of the Kings.

New Orleans hadn't been a good team in recent years. And so far in the new season, wins had been hard to come by. The previous night, New Orleans played against the Portland Trail Blazers. Anthony scored 31 points and grabbed 11 **rebounds**. The Pelicans had been ahead by 16 points. But Portland came back to win. "We've got to play better with the lead," Anthony said later.

From 1988 to 2002, the Pelicans played in Charlotte, North Carolina. Their nickname was the Hornets.

Anthony *(right)* defends the basket from a shot by Darren Collison.

Ryan Anderson *(right)* congratulates Anthony *(center)* after Anthony scored in the fourth quarter.

Against the Kings, Anthony played like a superstar for the second night in a row. He scored 28 points and came up with nine rebounds. He added two **steals** and three **blocks**. More important, the Pelicans played better with the lead. They won the game, 106–100.

The 2014–2015 season marked Anthony's third year in the NBA. It was also the second year in a row that he was voted to the All-Star Game. The big man was turning into a star, and the

Anthony's hard work on the court has drawn as much attention from fans as his trademark eyebrows have!

fans were excited. "People are starting to see all the hard work and dedication that I've been putting in," Anthony said. New Orleans coach Monty Williams thought Anthony deserved the attention. Anthony is "certainly one of the best players in the NBA," Williams said.

Anthony poses for a photo with his father, Anthony Sr. *(far left)*, and his mother, Erainer, in 2012.

PLAYING FOR FUN

Anthony Marshon Davis Jr. was born on March 11, 1993, in Chicago, Illinois. His parents are Anthony Sr. and Erainer. Anthony has a twin sister named Antoinette and an older sister named Iesha.

Anthony is older than Antoinette, his twin sister, by about one minute.

Anthony grew up in Englewood, an area on the Southwest Side of Chicago, Illinois.

The Davises lived in the Englewood neighborhood of Chicago. Many people who live there don't have much money. Young people often join street gangs and sell illegal drugs. "[Our neighborhood] was just surrounded by a lot of gang activities, shooting, violence," said Anthony Sr. "That was [Anthony's] first home."

Englewood boasts a strong basketball tradition. NBA players such as Derrick Rose grew up in the neighborhood. Playing sports is a way for people in Englewood to take their minds away from the violence around them. Young basketball players start **pickup games** with friends and play for local schools.

Derrick Rose *(right)* also grew up in Englewood. He plays for the Chicago Bulls.

Anthony loved basketball. He practiced with the hoop in his backyard. He often played there with friends from the neighborhood. He also played against his sister Iesha. "She used to always beat me, and that hurt," Anthony said. "She really taught me a lot about basketball, though."

Pickup games are easy to find in the neighborhood where Anthony grew up.

In 2004, Anthony and Antoinette began sixth grade at Perspectives Charter School. Erainer and Anthony Sr. had chosen Perspectives for their children because it could provide a good education. There was just one problem: the school didn't have a gym. Students used to shoot baskets outside on the blacktop. But that area had been turned into a parking lot.

Anthony didn't mind that his new school was focused on education and not sports. "I wasn't going there because of basketball," Anthony said. "My dream was always to go to college."

While Perspectives didn't have a gym, it did have a high school basketball team. They played home games on a court in a building at nearby Taylor Park. The conditions weren't ideal. Sometimes the roof leaked, and games had to be moved or canceled.

Anthony *(right)* drives the ball down the court during a Perspectives game in December 2010.

GETTING SERIOUS

As a freshman in 2007–2008, Anthony stood about 6 feet tall. He played **guard** for Perspectives. He dribbled smoothly and could sink outside shots. Anthony worked out with his cousins Keith, Jarvis, and Marshaun. The four boys practiced **drills** to help Anthony improve his quickness and **dribbling**.

Anthony also worked hard in the classroom. He made the honor roll at Perspectives. But his hard work on and off the court wasn't being noticed by college **scouts**. Playing for a team with a losing record made it hard for Anthony to get attention. He was also just 6 feet 3 inches tall. That isn't especially tall for a basketball player.

Scouts look for talented players to join college or professional teams.

After his junior year, Anthony had only one **scholarship** offer. It was from Cleveland State, a school that didn't have a winning men's basketball team. Anthony wasn't sure he had a future in the sport. "I didn't feel like playing," he said. "I just thought basketball wasn't for me."

In the summer of 2010, Anthony began to grow more quickly. He reached 6 feet 4 and then 6 feet 5. Midway through the summer, he stretched to 6 feet 6 and kept growing.

Anthony's growth spurt gave him confidence to keep playing basketball.

The change was stunning and obvious. "His feet were dangling off the bed," Erainer said. Clothes Anthony's mother had just bought for him were suddenly too short.

MeanStreets Basketball is a group that organizes games for top young players around the country. That summer, MeanStreets invited Anthony to play for their 17-and-under team. He

Derrick Rose played for MeanStreets in 2006. In the 2008–2009 season, he was named NBA Rookie of the Year.

still wasn't excited about basketball. But Anthony Sr. convinced his son to give it a try. The MeanStreets coaches also encouraged Anthony to stick with basketball. "I started taking it seriously, started playing," Anthony said. "The rest is history."

Anthony and his coaches took advantage of his growth spurt. They added new skills to his game, such as blocking.

6 FEET 10 INCHES

As Anthony grew taller, the way he played basketball changed. The MeanStreets coaches wanted him to play closer to the basket. That way, he could use his new height to better advantage. Anthony needed a whole new set of skills to play near the basket. But it didn't take long for him to feel comfortable as a forward. He still had the quick feet and shooting ability he had worked on as a guard. But now he had the height to block shots and grab rebounds too.

By the beginning of Anthony's senior year at Perspectives, he stood 6 feet 10. He had grown an incredible seven inches in less than a year! His parents bought him an extra-long, king-size bed.

Anthony's parents were concerned that their son was growing too quickly. They took him to a doctor, but Anthony was completely healthy.

Anthony's height and basketball ability made him stand out. He started receiving attention from college scouts and coaches all around the country.

He had quickly become one of the top-ranked high school players in the United States. In August 2010, Anthony decided he would go to the University of Kentucky after high school. He looked forward to working with coach John Calipari. "[Coach Calipari] will not tell me what I want to hear, but what I need to hear to improve," Anthony said.

Before he started college, Anthony played his final season at Perspectives. The excitement surrounding Anthony's future created a challenge for the school. Suddenly, lots of people wanted to watch Perspectives play. Vinay Mullick was the **athletic director** at the school in 2010. "[Anthony] was a big fish in a very, very small pond," Mullick said.

Luckily, Perspectives had moved their home games to a gym at the Illinois Institute of

Anthony was chosen to play in the McDonald's All-American Game in March 2011.

Technology (IIT) for the 2010–2011 season. Playing at IIT allowed more people to see Anthony play. And as a bonus, the roof didn't leak as it had at the old gym at Taylor Park. Anthony put on a show on his new court. He scored 32 points and snagged 18 rebounds per game in 2010–2011. He was ready for Kentucky.

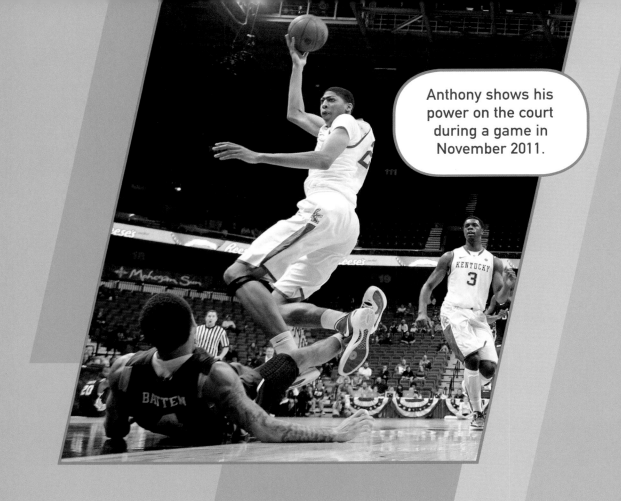

Anthony shows his power on the court during a game in November 2011.

YEAR OF THE WILDCAT

Anthony hadn't won a lot of games as a high school player. But that changed in a big way when he joined the Kentucky Wildcats for the 2011–2012 season. The team lost only two games all year. They stormed through the **National Collegiate Athletic Association (NCAA)** basketball **tournament**. In the championship game, the Wildcats beat the University of Kansas, 67–59. Anthony and his teammates were national champions!

Anthony had racked up more than 14 points and 10 rebounds per game in 2011–2012.

Anthony drives against Kansas during the NCAA tournament in 2012.

He had also blocked nearly five shots per game. The big man won a bunch of awards after the season. He was named Player of the Year by the Associated Press (AP). He won the John R. Wooden Award,

given each year to the best player in men's college basketball. He also took home the Naismith Men's College Player of the Year Award.

Anthony poses for photos with his Player of the Year award from the Associated Press.

On April 17, 2012, Anthony and some of his teammates announced that they were leaving Kentucky to join the NBA. Then, on June 28, the New Orleans Hornets chose Anthony with the first overall pick in the NBA **draft**. During his rookie season in 2012–2013, he scored 13.5 points and snared 8.2 rebounds per game.

Anthony hugs his mom after being drafted by the Hornets.

The Hornets changed their nickname to the Pelicans before the 2013–2014 season. Anthony totaled 20.8 points and 10 rebounds per game in his new uniform. He also blocked 2.8 shots per game, the best rate in the NBA. The league's coaches voted Anthony to the All-Star Game for the first time.

Anthony jumps for a slam dunk during the NBA All-Star Game on February 16, 2014.

Off the court, Anthony enjoys helping those in need and meeting fans at events.

Anthony has come a long way from his days playing basketball with his sister in their backyard. As a pro athlete, he can help people in need. Throughout the season, Anthony takes part in events such as serving meals to hungry people. "I'm trying to brighten up their day, make them feel special," Anthony said.

Anthony has already proven that he is a special basketball player. In the 2014–2015 season, he was voted to his second All-Star Game in a row. With Anthony leading the way, the Pelicans are a force in the NBA.

Anthony *(center)* celebrates with coach Monty Williams *(left)* and teammate Tyreke Evans after the Pelicans secured a spot in the 2015 playoffs.

Selected Career Highlights

2014–2015   Voted to the NBA All-Star Game for the
second time

2013–2014   Averaged 20.8 points, 10 rebounds,
and 2.8 blocks per game for
New Orleans
Led the NBA in blocks per game
Voted to the NBA All-Star Game for the
first time
Won a gold medal with Team USA at the
FIBA World Cup

2012–2013   Averaged 13.5 points, 8.2 rebounds, and 1.8 blocks
per game for New Orleans
Named to the NBA All-Rookie Team

2011–2012   Helped Kentucky win the national championship
Named the Final Four Most Outstanding Player
Won the John R. Wooden Award
Named AP Men's College Basketball Player of the Year
Won the Naismith Men's College Player of the Year Award
Chosen by the Pelicans as the first pick in the NBA draft
Won a gold medal with Team USA at the Olympic Games in
London

2010–2011   Grew seven inches between his junior and senior years
Scored 32 points and 18 rebounds per game for
Perspectives

Glossary

athletic director: the person in charge of all sports at a school

blocks: when players knock balls away to prevent the other team from scoring

draft: a yearly event in which teams take turns choosing new players from a group

dribbling: advancing the ball by bouncing it

drills: exercises meant to help improve at something

forward: a player on a basketball team who usually plays close to the basket

guard: a player on a basketball team who usually plays away from the basket

National Collegiate Athletic Association (NCAA): the group that oversees college basketball

pickup games: games among friends that aren't organized in advance

rebounds: balls grabbed after missed shots

rim: the metal hoop that a player must throw the ball through to score

rookie: a first-year player

scholarship: money awarded to students to help pay for college

scouts: basketball experts who watch players closely to judge their abilities

steals: plays that take possession of the ball from the other team

tournament: a set of games held to decide the best team

Further Reading & Websites

Fishman, Jon M. *Derrick Rose*. Minneapolis: Lerner Publications, 2015.

Gitlin, Marty. *Playing Pro Basketball*. Minneapolis: Lerner Publications, 2015.

Kennedy, Mike, and Mark Stewart. *Swish: The Quest for Basketball's Perfect Shot*. Minneapolis: Millbrook Press, 2009.

NBA
http://www.nba.com
The NBA's official website provides fans with recent news stories, statistics, biographies of players and coaches, and information about games.

Sports Illustrated Kids
http://www.sikids.com
The *Sports Illustrated Kids* website covers all sports, including basketball.

Index

Photo Acknowledgments

The images in this book are used with the permission of: © Kelley L Cox/
USA TODAY, pp. 4, 6; AP Photo/Rich Pedroncelli, pp. 5, 7; AP Photo/Don Ryan,
p. 8; © Charles Bertram/Lexington Herald-Leader/MCGetty Images, p. 9;
© iStockphoto.com/Paul Velgos, p. 10; Brian Kersey/UPI/Newscom, p. 11;
© Melanie Stetson Freeman/The Christian Science Monitor/Getty Images,
p. 12; © Warren Skalski/Chicago Tribune/TNS/Getty Images, p. 14; Brian
Kersey/UPI/Newscom, p. 15; © Anne Ryan/zrImages/CORBIS, pp. 16, 18; AP
Photo/Brian Kersey, p. 21; © Mark Cornelison/Lexington Herald-Leader/
MCT/Getty Images, pp. 22, 23; © Charles Bertram/Lexington Herald-Leader/
MCT/Getty Images, p. 24; Mike Segar/Reuters/Newscom, p. 25; © Christian
Petersen/Getty Images, p. 26; © Ilya S. Savenok/Getty Images for Samsung,
p. 27; © Stacy Revere/Getty Images, pp. 28, 29.

Front cover: © Stacy Revere/Getty Images.

Main body text set in Caecilia LT Std 55 Roman 16/28.
Typeface provided by Adobe Systems.